MLIQ1 QƆQᴸᴬᴼ

LIVING WITH SOBRIETY:
Another Beginning

Al-Anon Family Group Headquarters, Inc.
World Service Office for Al-Anon and Alateen
New York, N.Y. 1994

The Al-Anon Family Groups are a fellowship of relatives and friends of alcoholics who share their experience, strength and hope in order to solve their common problems. We believe alcoholism is a family illness and that changed attitudes can aid recovery.

Al-Anon is not allied with any sect, denomination, political entity, organization or institution; does not engage in any controversy, neither endorses nor opposes any cause. There are no dues for membership. Al-Anon is self-supporting through its own voluntary contributions.

Al-Anon has but one purpose: to help families of alcoholics. We do this by practicing the Twelve Steps, by welcoming and giving comfort to families of alcoholics, and by giving understanding and encouragement to the alcoholic.

The Suggested Preamble to the Twelve Steps

For information and catalog of literature write to
The World Service Office for Al-Anon and Alateen:

Al-Anon Family Group Headquarters, Inc.
P.O. Box 862   Midtown Station
New York, New York 10018-0862
212-302-7240   Fax 212-869-3757

This booklet is also available in: Finnish, Flemish, French, German, Italian, Portuguese and Spanish, and on audio cassette.

ISBN 0-910034-58-3

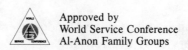 Approved by
World Service Conference
Al-Anon Family Groups

Table of Contents

"Sometimes it is good to look back—not to stare—just to learn."

BEGINNING AGAIN

Looking Back

For a brief moment, think of the energy used in demanding, begging, praying for someone else's sobriety. Remember the time spent thinking of logical arguments, loving reasons, imagined plans for someone else's sobriety.

Now, considering all that effort and time, how is it possible to be anything but relieved, grateful and content when at long last he, or she, is sober? Having remembered the havoc which problem drinking brought to the alcoholic and those close to him, or her, why isn't it enough just to witness the miracle of sobriety? After the years of anger and fear, recriminations and regrets, the loss of health, the financial insecurity, the emotional distress, the loss of faith—after all that, why isn't sobriety the end of the long search for those who love someone who suffers from the disease of alcoholism?

The members of the Al-Anon Family Groups, Al-Anon and Alateen, know from sharing their experience, strength and hope at meetings that there is more to recovering from the effects of alcoholism than living with sobriety. We know from our experience that alcoholism is a family disease, that compulsive drinking has affected those closest to the alcoholic: friends and family. By the time sobriety comes to the one we love, our heads are still full of the remembrances of watchful waiting; our emotions are packed with anger and leftover resentments; our spirits are weighed down by the broken promises and the absence of trust. Almost everything about us has been altered by our reactions to drinking situations. These effects on our behavior, so often subtle and insidious, were years in the making and won't disappear just because someone else stops drinking.

5

While we can rejoice with each other over the end of the drinking and the chance for a new beginning, we also know that along with sobriety's joys and pleasant surprises—there can be difficulties. We may need help to begin again.

The alcoholic can also be a potential victim of the past. To better understand the nature of the disease, it should be stated that alcoholism isn't cured by sobriety; it is only arrested. Alcoholics cannot drink alcohol in any form, or their progressive disease can become full blown once again and the characteristics and habit patterns of the drinking days seldom dissolve just because alcohol is removed from the body. Our friends in Alcoholics Anonymous tell us that the three-fold disease of alcoholism has affected the drinker, mentally, physically and spiritually, and that in order to stay sober, alcoholics must put sobriety above everything because, without it, there will be nothing but eventual madness and/or death. Those are very powerful reasons for alcoholics to concentrate on not drinking. To do that, they may still need help.

It isn't easy for anyone in an alcoholic situation to begin again. Just the thought of trying can be exhausting to those who still suffer from the fatigue of past experience. In looking at the needs of the entire family, including the recovering alcoholic, it would seem that before we could have a new and happy life, together or apart, we would all have to find a way somehow to put the past to rest.

Not everyone is willing or able to do so. Some of us choose not to consider someone else's sobriety as an opportunity to start again. Our pain is too deep, all encompassing; we have lost any feeling we might have had for the alcoholic. There are those of us who only live with a recovering alcoholic because we are financially unable to leave. Yet, there are many in favor of trying again; some are sure and confident, others, cautious and watchful.

Sometimes the most confident among us become discouraged with the new problems sobriety brings. We express dismay at the amount of change which we feel is required in our own lives as a result of living with someone who cannot drink. We think the alcoholic's recovery process, the meetings and friends, appear to be more important than we are. We speak of new fears, new feelings of guilt. We think we don't communicate well, that we don't know what to say to the alcoholic, or how to say it. For some, there is always the lingering, haunting fear that if we say or do the wrong thing, the alcoholic might just pick up that first drink again.

We know there isn't much use in cataloging a list of complaints about living with sobriety, but we also know there isn't much to be gained by denying the problems or refusing to discuss them. One of the most helpful aspects of the Al-Anon/Alateen fellowship is the opportunity we have to voice our dilemmas, confident that we won't be condemned for speaking frankly. Instead, we usually hear how others have used the tools of the program, the slogans, the Steps, and the Traditions to deal with similar feelings and situations. It is in this sharing we gain the strength to improve our attitudes and our lives.

Looking Forward

It has also been our experience that there are many members of the Al-Anon/Alateen fellowship who have managed to cope with most of the difficulties which sobriety presents, and live happily by:

accepting the changes brought about by sobriety;

recognizing and reducing their resentments and feelings of guilt;

dealing with their disappointments;

increasing their capacity to communicate; and

learning how to be happy through spiritual growth in the Al-Anon program.

We offer here, then, the thoughts and reflections on living with sobriety of the Al-Anon family today: wives, husbands, friends, men, women, children, the married and unmarried. There are thoughts from those who feel their efforts were worthwhile and, those who were disappointed. Their reactions are as varied as their experiences. In offering their views, they make no attempt

7

to tell others what to do; they state simply and directly what they have done under a given set of circumstances. All have lived with sobriety and most have lived with active alcoholism. Many first hoped that joining Al-Anon or Alateen would help their loved ones get sober, only to discover a greater understanding of the value of living one day at a time in Al-Anon. They discovered that their own happiness did not depend on the absence of alcoholic intoxication; rather, it lay in concentrating on using the tools of the program to reach for personal recovery, emotional maturity and spiritual peace.

". . . Everyone agreed it was going to be different."

ACCEPTING THE CHANGES

Sometimes our enthusiasm for change depends on our willingness to take a chance on tomorrow by risking what we have today. Often, that willingness for us is subject to the amount of damage done to our relationships during the drinking years. Our incentive to try again may have to warm up to the promise of a better life to come, having suffered from the chilling effects of broken promises and misplaced trust. For some, the risk may be too great. But for those of us who are willing to try, there will be changes to accept.

For many of us, sobriety is a welcome alternative to active alcoholism; the atmosphere is more quiet, there is less fighting, meals may be eaten together and on time, the bills are being paid, there is hopeful talk and plans are being made.

For others, living with sobriety is a bit more complicated. Some of us may have lost more than the problem drinker.

Often we feel a loss of self-esteem: Praised by family and friends for our loving and dogged determination to stay with the alcoholic under the worst conditions, we are reduced to watching the non-drinking loved one gather in the congratulations for not doing something. The sober alcoholic appears to continue to be the main attraction, the one who receives all the attention, the "strong" noble one.

There are other feelings of loss. Life seems to have less meaning, new friends command the attention we would like to receive from a newly-sobered loved one. Others have taken over the role of lifesaver, companion and soul mate. While our loved ones pursue recovery by going to meetings without us, we may feel lonely.

We may seem to have less to do. Where every waking minute

had become part of our intense battle against alcohol, now our time stretches in front of us. The alcoholic is busy in recovery, and we are left to fill our lives with something other than thinking about the drinking. We may feel bored.

We may lose our scapegoat, the drinking—the reason we were always angry, couldn't do our work, failed to achieve our own successes, neglected friendships, and we are left with a residue of unresolved conflicts and nothing to blame for the way we feel.

We may no longer know what to expect in the way of behavior. Everything about the alcoholic seems to change; those who used to stay home, go out; those once-shy, turn independent; sleepers wake; agnostics pray—habits, appetites, attitudes—*everything* changes.

We may change. Some of us may react to all these changes with anger and/or fear. We may wonder how we are going to get through all the stages and phases, the levels of growth and recovery. Changes seem threatening, almost unwelcome, and our feelings are mixed because we really do want our lives to progress, we do want to be secure and relieved, loving and loved.

One of the ways we are able to accept change is with the help of others. Knowing we are not alone often quiets our fears, and helps us gain perspective. As our fears lessen, we can begin to concentrate on the damage that the drinking has done to us and allow the alcoholic to pursue continued sobriety without our resentment and anger. As we gain spiritual strength, we can begin to accept and even to welcome the changes sobriety brings.

REFLECTIONS ON

New Sobriety: I was so thrilled when he came home from his first AA meeting. I tried to do everything his doctor, his counselor and his AA sponsor suggested. I didn't nag, complain or bring up old resentments about his drinking days. I believed, and still do, that he was suffering from a disease, and that his recovery would be made easier if I could be confident, cheerful and kind.

I worked hard to keep out of his way and let him take over responsibilities when he thought he was able to. I didn't press him to go out or to parties, I let him decide if we should have liquor in the house. I made hearty meals and kept my voice low and affectionate. I kept this up for months until one day I thought I would explode. He was doing fine—I was getting worse. I finally went to Al-Anon to get help in dealing with my lingering fears and bottled-up anger. It was a relief to have people I could talk to about *me* for a change.

Special Attention: I was emotionally exhausted by sobriety. I allowed the alcoholic to be the "star" in the drinking days and I made the same mistake when she began her recovery. I treated her like a fragile saint when she stopped drinking. I gave her so much time and extra attention that my daughter said, "Boy, it really pays to be sick around here." What she was telling me was that *everyone* in an alcoholic situation deserves and needs extra loving care. Al-Anon has shown me the need for trying to give *equal* attention to lessen the damaging effects of the disease on *all* of us.

Pink Clouds: I was overjoyed by my wife's sobriety. It was great not to sit in my office worrying about what was going on at home. I began to relax. I explained to the children that their mother needed understanding while her sobriety was so new and I ran to Al-Anon with every question about her recovery. Members were very patient with my "pink cloud" phase but I wasn't as patient with those who said they were having trouble living with sobriety. I said, "How ungrateful can you be? He, or she is sober, right? Anything is better than living with a drunk, isn't it?" My sponsor explained that members had a right to express themselves; they were trying to recover by being truthful, admitting their doubts and trying to handle their disappointments. These same people were the ones who helped me when my pink cloud burst! Tired of having to say the "right thing" to my sober-but-touchy wife, I was asking everyone, "How long is this recovery of hers going to take?'' Only then, did I begin to understand what they all had been trying to tell me; Al-Anon was where *my* recovery was going to take place.

Changing Attitudes: I felt I had lost something when my mom got sober. I never liked being the daughter of a drunk but I was *used* to it. The fights, the shouting, having something to worry about, even always knowing I was expected to do all the work, were familiar things I could count on. I was never bored; knowing about the drinking behavior seemed better than not knowing how her sobriety would turn out.

I began to feel better when I accepted the fact that living with sobriety had to be different from living with an active alcoholic. No one in Alateen could guarantee that it was going to be *better,* but everyone agreed that it was going to be *different.* If I wanted a better life, I would first have to adjust to change.

Live and Let Live: I wanted my wife to get sober. I knew she was a fine, sensitive person who had so much to offer, if only she wouldn't drink. She had been sober for some time when, in a fight, I heard myself shouting, ''You might as well drink, you're impossible sober!'' I spoke to my sponsor about her lack of willingness to do what I thought was reasonable. Sure, I wanted her sober but I wanted her sober *my* way. This new, outspoken woman wasn't the shy, pliable person I had married. When my sponsor responded with a loud ''live and let live'' I had to do a lot of thinking. My wife was entitled to make her own way. I would have to accept this idea if we were going to have a new life together.

Forgetting about Blame: Losing a target for all our family troubles was a real shock. For a long time, I couldn't admit that I was the cause of any difficulty. After all, hadn't *he* done all the drinking? When he joined AA, he was growing up—I was standing still, self-righteous and miserable. There was no one to blame anymore for the way I felt.

Trusting Again: It may not be easier but *relating* to a sober person is better than *dealing* with a drunk. Sober people may object to our plans and suggestions and can resist taking the blame when something goes wrong: What used to be a "dead body" now walks around noticing things, offering advice and issuing commands. But, unless that spirit comes to life, what have you got? Nothing! For me, my life with my father began to get better when I decided a sober person is more likely to be reliable, and reliability is the basis of trust. I decided to trust in Dad's desire to get well and use my energy to fix the damage done to *me* by the disease.

Letting Go: At first I was glad to give up the martyr role of lifesaver. Then I wasn't so sure. I resented the men who came to take my wife to meetings. Later, when I became convinced that I should leave her recovery to the "experts"—other sober alcoholics, her doctor, etc., I finally had the time to look after my own time-table for recovery and let her do what she needed to for herself.

Using Detachment: I had worked at "detaching" when my younger sister was drinking. I thought I understood how to let her live her own emotional ups and downs without sharing her reactions. Using detachment with a sober person hadn't occurred to me. I was really playing "big brother" and hovering over her. Recognizing the limits of my responsibility helped me gain the perspective we both needed to build a new and valuable friendship.

Taking the First Step: Remembering I was powerless over anything but my own life and attitudes helped me accept my husband's treatment. Through members in the program, I learned that his recovery was his exclusive job and I could choose to accept his needs without being overwhelmed by them. He drank carloads of coffee and soda; he wanted to go to *one* meeting and then *ten* meetings a week; he wanted to take over the bill-paying but let the bills pile up until they spilled over; he was deaf to the dripping faucets and blind to the broken windows; he wanted to talk, talk, talk while I listened, listened, LISTENED! I wasn't sure if I should object—when what he needed wasn't what *I* really needed or wanted. Whose recovery comes first? Is the sickest, first? Who's more sick? Was something I said or did less important? I decided on a course of action for my recovery. I did what I needed to do first. I wasn't rude or unkind but firm in my own mind. Now, by taking the First Step every day, I am working on developing my own character and sense of well-being while giving him the freedom to do the same.

Reassessing Responsibility:
What I do or don't do does not make another person an alcoholic.

What I do or don't do does not make another person sober.

What I do or don't do does not make another person stay sober.

What I do or don't do *makes me who I am* and I have a primary responsibility to myself: to make myself into the best person I can possibly be. Then, and only then, will I have something worthwhile to share.

Helping: If one person gets well, the whole family situation improves and even the alcoholic can benefit from the changed family attitudes. In the same way, the family benefits when the alcoholic gets help. The more people who work on recovery, the better! It is to the entire family's advantage to understand and encourage the method of recovery chosen by the alcoholic while not accepting the responsibility, the blame or the credit for the results.

My family has developed a hands-off policy toward the alcoholic's recovery. We try to be supportive and cooperative and then get out of the way. Even though the recovery may take a long time, we're willing to wait. My wife didn't become an alcoholic overnight—she's not going to get well immediately. Neither are we. On the other hand, I recognize that she may never become easy to live with, although she's sober. It's my choice to look at my own circumstances and make my own decisions. No one in Al-Anon tells me to stay or leave, and I'm grateful for that.

Concentrating on Oneself: I asked, "If the alcoholic concentrates solely on recovering from alcoholism and the non-alcoholic concentrates on recovering from the effects of the disease, how do we ever get together? If and when we do, will we like each other? Will we love each other? If adjusting to the sober state requires so much work by the family and friends toward acceptance, changed attitudes, a shift in responsibilities—why not just dump all the problems and get out?" My questions were answered at a meeting when a member asked me, "Can you go without bringing yourself along?"

Then I knew that for me, running would have been a disaster. I was so damaged by the time I got to the Al-Anon program I couldn't have made it with him, or without him, without help.

Friends: I worried about what I could tell my friends. I had told most of them how bad it was during the drinking days and I wanted to tell them my mother had joined AA, but I had heard about protecting her anonymity. I didn't know what to do. I wanted them to know that she wasn't hopeless, that she had joined a recovery program. I wanted to be rid of the guilt I felt about telling friends all our family secrets. My new Alateen friends suggested that what I had thought and said in the past couldn't be erased by telling all today. They said I could learn to forgive and forget the ugly things I had said about my mother, that they were said in bad times, under difficult circumstances. Then I found a way to handle her anonymity and mine. What I did say to my friends was that I had found a program of recovery in Alateen. They were free to ask me anything they wanted to know about *me*, but I wasn't free to answer questions about my mother.

Parents: I did so want my parents to understand about my husband's sobriety. I tried every way I could to make them appreciate AA and Al-Anon but they seemed oblivious. They constantly brought up the past; either insisted that he have "just one drink," or they wouldn't offer him anything saying, "Oh, I forgot you don't want any." They seemed to be waiting for the day when they *knew* he would drink again.

At my meetings I discussed their resistance to these changes. Others shared how they had learned to use the program with loved ones who weren't alcoholic. Members reminded me that I couldn't change my parents but I could learn to accept their fondness for the certainties of the past. I could detach and still love them without sharing their doubts in our programs. I offered them the availability of Al-Anon and stopped trying to convince them. In time, they saw the change in both of us and decided things were better without my assurances.

Acquaintances: Most of our friends had given us both up as too-troubled-to-know. Invitations had all but stopped and at first, I thought sobriety only made things worse. The few times we were invited out, *I* drank more than I wanted to. Embarrassed and ill at ease, I felt someone should have something to drink so we wouldn't look out-of-place because she wasn't drinking. Once she insisted that I have a drink and while I didn't want one, I agreed. Later, I worked out a new set of social rules for myself: I didn't have to drink unless I wanted to; I needn't make excuses for her, or answer for her drinking or not drinking; I could enjoy the company of nondrinkers, too. Because we lived together, we made joint decisions about serving liquor when we started to entertain, but I still exercised my own decisions in social situations. We have a new set of friends today, more than I ever expected. Many of them are program people with more to offer than I had ever hoped.

Changing: I remember saying that it would be wonderful if the recovering alcoholic in my life really worked the spiritual program

offered in AA; saw sobriety as a new beginning, forgot old resentments, forgave mistakes, recognized that I was a victim of
the disease of alcoholism, too; understood that I needed help in
recovering from living with the active drinking days; treated me
with consistent courtesy, kindness and patience; was always fair,
generous and loving; resisted anger, deceit, anxiety and moody
behavior; avoided self-justification, self-pity, resentful criticism;
was open, honest and sharing; showed appreciation for my loyalty;
recovered totally—immediately—faster—I would have settled for
soon! What a list! And do you know what my sponsor told me?
She said it would be wonderful if we could be all the things we
think others should be; that I would do well to accept the challenge
to look to my own recovery before I spent anymore of my precious
life wishing the alcoholic would change into someone I could be
glad to live with, or, even someone I could stand to live with.

"Our worries don't end just because the drinking stops."

COURAGE

Fear is a natural emotion. Most people would agree that it is wise to be afraid of some things; traffic and lions take their toll of fearless victims, but being afraid constantly is not good for most of us. Some of us suffer from nervous disorders, twitches, rashes, and unexplainable headaches that are noticeably evident when our tensions increase. Our pressures and anxieties don't disappear just because we are living with sobriety.

Some of us who managed to conquer our worries during the drinking days were surprised by a new set of fears with sobriety. This fear is often expressed in the questions, "What will I do if he drinks again?" "What if I say or do the wrong thing, can I ruin his sobriety?" "What if she decides she doesn't love me when she's sober awhile?" "What if I decide I don't love him anymore?"

Gaining confidence in ourselves, learning to dispel our doubts, takes time and effort.

REFLECTIONS ON

First Things First: When my fears kept me from enjoying myself during the drinking days, my friends told me to do the things I needed to do to look human and survive: eat, brush my teeth, comb my hair. I remember feeling that the simplest accomplishments helped to remove some doubts. Later, I began to gain confidence and my fears were replaced by my growing self-esteem. I was genuinely surprised by a whole new set of fears in living

18

with sobriety. To conquer them, I went back to the slogans for comfort and support. When I found myself slipping into that old pattern of fear, I tried to do what I needed to do to get through the day. With or without sobriety, I had to work through my fear.

Easy Does It: I was always thinking, "Something has to be done about this!" I was so anxious, I never rose from my seat, I always jumped. I became more frantic with sobriety. I seemed to be the family's permanent volunteer. I even jumped to my feet at my meetings. A friend suggested that avoiding some pressures could lessen my anxiety. She said if I could find a way to reduce the load, I could reduce the strain. I knew that I was always trying to do too much but I didn't believe I could keep myself still. Her suggestion was for me to grab onto my chair and hold on while I asked myself, "Should I do this (whatever the activity was) today?" and "Should I be the one to do this?" In the time it took for me to ask these questions, I could see if anyone else wanted to volunteer. The first chance I had to practice restraint came on Christmas day. My husband's parents were coming for dinner and as I looked around the living room which was submerged in torn wrappings and bows, I struggled to keep myself sitting where I was. While I was asking those two suggested questions, my husband appeared with two children. *He* said, "Something has to be done about this, boys. We'd better pick this room up." When I thanked them all for their great job, they just beamed.

Easy Does It—But Do It: I wasn't the frenzied-action type. I was a sitter and I continued to sit and watch during sobriety. I was afraid to do anything, fearful of criticism and what others would think, especially my newly-sober mother. She was always telling people I was so good. When she drank, she thought I was such a quiet, good kid. She thought I didn't need Alateen but my Dad was less convinced. He asked me to attend at least six meetings and I went because I was afraid not to. It was such a relief to have a place where I could act my age. Oh, I guess I went a little wild at first, but I found a happy medium after awhile. I really needed to get up off my chair.

Doing Nothing: I meditate. I don't move or talk. I grind down the gears until all the actions which are motivated by fear come to a halt. I just sit still.

Thinking: I discipline my mind by trying to concentrate on one thing at a time. During the drinking days, my habit was to have distracted, racing thoughts and they were interrupted, panicky and without direction. I know now that my thinking is my responsibility, that fear gets in my way if I let my thoughts run wild.

Thinking of Positive Things: I try to reject all the negative thoughts that pop into my head and replace them with positive ones. Before Al-Anon, I found that my thinking leaned toward the critical, the negative. I guess it was part of that old pattern of denial and I had a hard time thinking happy thoughts. In the beginning, when someone gave me a way of improving myself, I would say, "yes, but." There was always some condition I placed on everything. Now that I concentrate on being positively willing to have courage, courage is part of my life.

Taking the Steps: When I became willing to believe in a Power greater than myself, I surrendered the fear that my wife would drink again. This serenity has been reinforced by my regular attendance at Al-Anon meetings. I took the Third Step and I began to live twenty-four hours at a time. In taking the Sixth Step, however, I made room for extra courage by getting ready to have some real defects removed from my character. By the time I took the Seventh Step, I was sure that I was giving up my fear and giving in to courage.

Doing the Thing I Fear: When my mother was drinking, I thought it was clever to tell people what I was afraid of. I thought it was "smart" to speak of being afraid of heights and closed spaces. I didn't know then that I was often a bore or, an attention-seeker. Later, when she was sober, and I found I had a real set of terrifying anxieties, I was helpless. I was genuinely afraid. To get better, I had to force myself to smile and step into a room full of people, even if they were Alateen people. Yet, their encouragement helped me get to meetings outside the safety of my home. Now, when I get the flutter in the pit of my stomach, I take a deep breath and make the effort to face the moment.

Conquering Jealousy: I was jealous of his AA friends. I had some very good cause, too: other women. They picked him up for meetings, called him at home, gave him presents, and sent him perfumed notes and cards. I hated and blamed them for stalking my husband. When my worst suspicions were confirmed, I became desperate. I blamed everyone but my husband, although I really knew he was enjoying himself, and I seemed to be the only one who was suffering. I agonized, "How could he do this to me? After all we have been through together, is he going to leave me for another woman?" I was in terrible pain, I loved him, I hated him. I hated myself. Al-Anon friends urged me not to take his behavior personally, to work the program and heal the wounds, to let my jealousy go by placing his care in the hands of my Higher Power. It took a great deal of time, many phone calls and meetings but I began to believe that my husband was the one who was missing something by deciding not to be with me. The busier I became with my Al-Anon work, the less obsessed I became with his behavior. I began to look better to myself and, I might add, I noticed that I was beginning to look good to others. Even my husband noticed the change in me; I wasn't desperate anymore. After a long separation my husband asked me to give our marriage another chance. I was able to say "yes" because I still cared for him and I knew I had put my jealousy to rest. He has matured in his sobriety and I still go to meetings to work on my spiritual growth and emotional stability. I think Al-Anon is helping me to become the kind of person any one would feel lucky to be with.

Rejection: I loved my wife, but she left me after several years of sobriety. I was hurt and frantic. I didn't know how I could manage to live without her. I was afraid of living alone and afraid to admit it. I didn't want to return to my bachelor days and I was worried about the kids; I felt totally deserted and abandoned. Al-Anon friends helped me get over the damage done to my ego. They suggested that I finally take a Fourth-Step inventory and see that I had some good points in my favor. They helped me get over my terrible loneliness by asking me to reach out to help others who were more lonely than I. I made "Twelfth Step" my middle name. I became involved in Al-Anon service work and traveled through the Area, meeting new friends, developing new interests. What a difference it made in my life!

Facing Reality: I live apart from a sober alcoholic, but I still come to Al-Anon. All the people I deal with in my everyday life are sober, but I was so used to living with a drinker that I didn't have much practice dealing with people who thought rationally. When I started working to support myself, I was surprised and annoyed by logical thinking. I had become such a con-artist, too. I was so afraid of the alcoholic in his drinking days that I had learned to duck and weave emotionally, as well as physically. When I took a good look at my attitudes, I didn't like what I saw. I sounded confident but I was afraid to admit a single mistake. I couldn't stand criticism and I had become very good at lying. Reality, living on my own, scared me. Now when I speak to my sponsor, I practice sticking to the facts and listening without making excuses for my behavior.

I feel better about myself every day. I know I cannot blame these defects on an alcoholic, drunk or sober. These are my flaws, and mine to correct. Alcoholism may have pushed them to the surface but they were in me and if I want to recover, I had to deal with them.

Living on my Own: Both my parents are sober now. Legally, I was considered an adult, but when I moved out of my parents' home, I was really worried. Could I make it on my own? Well, through Al-Anon, I gained the courage I needed. I am no longer afraid of being alone. I am free to develop at my own rate, in my own way. I am free to move when and where I choose, entertain whom I please, read, go to school, exercise, pay attention to my appearance and my health. I'm not afraid of growing up.

Single Parenthood: Living alone with the children frightened me. But like everything else, it wasn't impossible. My children are great company and good fun. Some attend Alateen and use their program to get over the resentments they have toward me and their father. I have to be the disciplinarian, the breadwinner, the leader, and sometimes I get in their way. I resented their anger toward me in the beginning, but Al-Anon members helped me admit that the kids had been hurt by the disease and by my reactions to it. I respect my children as individuals. They deserve to be treated with dignity, kindness and respect. I see them in a different light. They are not such a burden, rather they are my reminders of what it is to be young. Because of their ages, I am responsible for them and they need me to try to be at my best. They respect me as a person, too. They see me go to meetings; they help me work my program by reminding me when I slip and use my mouth instead of my brain. They have their own relationships with their father, I keep out of those. "Live and let live," applies to children too.

"Patience comes with acceptance."

RESENTMENTS

Anger, like the other human emotions, has its place in our lives. It can be a form of self-protection, a sign to others that our frustration level has been reached, that our person is being offended, that we will not accept the unacceptable. Like other passions, it can swing out of control, and while we would be less than human if we did without it, we would be equally inhuman if we lived in a perpetual state of rage.

Many people who are living with recovering alcoholics say they have trouble with their own anger; they have none or they have too much. They have problems with the alcoholic's anger too; they don't like it, they don't think they should have to tolerate it, but they don't know what to do about it. Most agree that old resentments and new frustrations tend to decrease the possibilities for pleasant living. Uncontrollable anger can make our lives unmanageable and often propel us into taking another person's inventory. It can make us forget that we are powerless to change others and can get in the way of recognizing our own recovery needs. Having no anger at all, points to a lack of self-esteem. Gaining balance between the two extremes appears to be one solution.

REFLECTIONS ON

Recognizing Anger: I forgot what it was like to be truly angry. My early frustrations and rages during the drinking years were hammered into desperate hopelessness. I couldn't get angry any-

24

more. I felt I deserved the painful life I was leading. I had no self-worth, couldn't take any kind of argument, would do anything for peace. On top of that, I had been coached from childhood to believe that anger was unrefined and unladylike. At meetings, I claimed to be unfamiliar with anger: I never shouted, I never hit my children in a rage. I never did much of anything, but cry. My husband was not drinking, he was going to AA, and I cried and cried and cried. Someone asked me to consider that my depression might be anger turned inward. I knew I was tired of my own tears so I said the Serenity Prayer hundreds of times a day, until I could say out loud, "That makes me angry!" and detach from his reactions to what I said. What a relief it was to stop those tears.

Being Straightforward: I had hidden facts from my wife when she was drinking and I continued to hide bills, broken toys, even our son's grades when she got sober. I just didn't want to hear all the noise she made over bad news; she seemed angry enough for the two of us. I couldn't stand all that yelling. While I wouldn't tell her she bothered me, I found myself letting her know I disapproved in more subtle ways: I forgot to do things when I said I would; I came home later than I said I'd be. Through the program, I took my inventory and discovered I was quietly trying to get even. My remedy was to allow both of us to be angry when we were, and to try to express myself honestly, no matter what the outcome.

Acceptance: I thought I was working the program by trying to be patient. I no longer think that patience is a remedy for resentful anger. Patience comes with an attitude of acceptance, not from holding back anger. I had to stop denying my anger and look at it squarely so I could do something about it. I have heard at Al-Anon that I am responsible for my own actions and thoughts, that other people do not make me do what I do, or think the way I think. I have accepted myself and I'm beginning to accept other people the way they are each day. Now, I have fewer resentments.

Disguised Anger: My daughter's sober behavior made me mad. It was harder to take than her noisy drinking days. It covered months of her silences, coldness, lack of interest and depression. I shouldn't have taken her inventory but I wanted to understand why she behaved that way so I could let it go and not get upset by her actions. Her withdrawal seemed the most difficult for me to deal with. I wanted to provoke a fight just to clear the air. Al-Anon friends helped me to concentrate on getting out of her head and to stop analyzing her behavior. I helped both of us when I said I was available if she wanted to talk, but stopped myself from asking questions about how she felt. Everything I said was a statement, even simple things, "There's coffee ready, if you want some." I also made my own life very busy.

Later she said she appreciated the fact that I no longer nagged her and I was glad to be free of my obsession with her well-being.

Letting Off Steam: I think there are acceptable ways for an adult to show anger and unless we can deal with gathering crowds, it isn't a good idea to scream and rage in the street. I try to let off steam before I get too close to the point where I want to hit someone or tear them apart with words. I also avoid the sober alcoholic when I think her mood is close to violent action. I feel I shouldn't be the victim and, on the other hand, I try not to add fuel to her fire. When I feel I am losing my temper, I leave the room in the middle of a sentence, if I have to, and call my sponsor or someone in the program. I let off steam to anyone who will listen, until the more violent anger is gone and I am in a better position to find an alternative way to solve my problems or get rid of my frustrations.

Acting, Not Reacting: I don't have to get angry just because someone else is. I don't have to raise my voice; a really angry person isn't going to hear what I yell back, anyway. It's foolish to fight physically with someone bigger, stronger, or who fights dirty, and it's plain dumb to fight if I don't want to. Old habit patterns are difficult to break. When I remembered drinking days so full of fights someone had picked as an excuse to get out of the house for a drink, I also remembered a word I'd heard used by members who didn't want to get involved in an argument. They would say, "Oh," "Oh!" or "OH?" Then, when the loud anger subsided, they were able to join in a longer, more meaningful conversation.

Marriage to a Sober Alcoholic: I attended a few meetings of Al-Anon before I married a recovering alcoholic but it didn't occur to me that the program should or would apply to me.

Soon after our marriage, I began feeling restricted. We couldn't seem to socialize as other young people did. It was hard to understand why my husband couldn't take even one drink. I grew resentful and frustrated. I asked myself, "Is this all there is to marriage?" I was desperate for answers. I went to Al-Anon.

A member of AA spoke at my Al-Anon meeting. He said once he stopped drinking he no longer suffered from the "alcoholic" part of his disease, but the "ism" part still remained. He said everyone used to say—back in his drinking days—that he was a prince of a fellow whenever he was sober. But he found out when he took his inventory that he had a great many defects. When I heard that, I realized that the sober alcoholic I had married was still working on becoming who he was and that was not necessarily the person I always dreamed he would be. I could count myself lucky because I hadn't had to live with the active drinking episodes but I was going to live with the emotional make-up that contributed to the illness in the first place. My answers were in Al-Anon. There I was able to work on my own character defects. With both of us working on a spiritual way of life, we have a better-than-average chance for a good marriage.

"Somehow, I thought it would be better."

DISAPPOINTMENTS

Many of our disappointments in living with sobriety can be measured by our expectations of it:

Some of us expected too much, attached magical wonders to sobriety, counted on it to solve all our problems, leaned on it to make us feel better about ourselves. We were disappointed.

Some of us expected too much too soon, forgot that alcoholism was a lifetime illness, that sobriety was only the beginning of recovery, that it could be short-lived, that our loved ones might still have character defects. We were disappointed.

Some of us had no expectations. Numb from battles we didn't start on battlegrounds we didn't choose, we no longer expected anything. We mistook the absence of pain for happiness. When we recognized our confusion, we were disappointed.

And then there were those of us who felt there was a difference between expectation and hope. While we tried not to count on things turning out well, we still hoped that sobriety might mean a certain togetherness, a sharing of experience and responsibilities, a pleasant life. Some of us were disappointed.

There is no end to life's difficult turns, and yet, does that mean we should be without hope? Don't we all know people who have supportive and helpful loved ones who still suffer their losses, poor health, or bad debts? Living with sobriety is, after all, living. As long as we live, we are going to be subject to life's disappointments as well as our own, and because we cannot hope to avoid them all, it appears we might do better to find a way to neutralize their damaging effects on us.

Some of us have managed to deal with disappointments by setting realistic goals, avoiding expectations of others, and using the Al-Anon program when, in spite of our best intentions, we were unsatisifed.

28

REFLECTIONS ON

Trying Not to Project: I tried to stop forecasting the future. No one knows how a situation will turn out, so why should I waste time expecting, that from a certain result, I will be joyous or desperate? When I stopped dwelling on how things would probably work out, I was better able to pay attention to what I was doing.

Boredom: My days seemed so empty, my nights so lonely, I couldn't imagine what I could do with myself while she went to all those meetings. All that time seemed to oppress me. I spent most of the hours as I had spent them before: waiting. I was waiting for her to come home, waiting for her to recover, waiting for her to do something so we could begin again. There was nothing for me to do, I thought, nothing. My sponsor really shocked me when he said, "Being bored is an excuse for being uninterested in life." I hadn't thought of boredom as a character defect before. Here I had prayed to be released from the pain of living with an active drinker, and I was unable to interest myself in any activity when she was sober. Of the three things I had always wanted to do but hadn't, I chose one; I began to play tennis again. I'm not ready for competition yet, but I feel wonderful.

Independence: We went to AA meetings *together;* I thought we were working the program *together*. I was so hurt when he said, "I don't want you to come to *my* meetings anymore. This is *my* program." First, I cried bitter tears of rejection; then I got angry. At my Al-Anon meeting I yelled, "What kind of a program divides *mine* and *yours?*" After my outburst, members offered their thoughts. In thinking, "first things first," one suggested that AA meetings were held by and for alcoholics. Non-alcoholics were welcome at open AA meetings by an unwritten invitation but if that invitation was withdrawn, it might be best to accept the situation. Another said I did have Al-Anon friends and other open

AA meetings available to me; still another suggested that my husband's independence could be a welcome attitude; it takes self-confidence to do things on your own and there would be a number of times in our lives which would require a growing self-reliance for both of us. I feel now that each of us is learning to be a new person and this is done best by not insisting on sharing every moment. I spent a good deal of time working on my disappointment at not being chosen as my husband's chief companion at meetings. In the meantime, I think we are actually getting closer in other ways because of our new sense of respect for one another.

Preoccupation with Recovery: I was alone more after she sobered up than when she was drinking. When we were together, all she talked about was alcoholism, AA and meetings. If I questioned her or showed annoyance, she countered with, "My sobriety comes first." As much as I knew that was true, I wondered how I was expected to live a solitary married life. I had always thought marriage meant some companionship as part of the commitment. I'm not sure which ran out first, her preoccupation, or my patience, but I did manage to be less resentful and had accepted a few social engagements with friends, telling her I was going out and she was welcome to join me if she liked. Today, there is room for AA, Al-Anon and many other activities. Her sobriety still comes first, but it isn't any longer the only topic of conversation.

Isolation: My Dad had been sober for three years when I told my group he was still rotten to live with. He never showed me any affection and he argued with me about everything—baseball scores, my car, my opinions—you name it. I wanted to love him, I wanted to just *like* him, but I couldn't get past his big mouth. I said I thought he was still "sick" although he wasn't drinking, that the situation would never change. I almost fell over when a skinny thirteen year old said, "So your Dad still has character defects, that's *his* problem, and if you think more about his defects than you do about yours, that's *your* problem." He was right. I was always thinking about the kind of father I wanted him to be. I even made up a fantasy father who told me I was a good kid and took me to a Grand Prix auto race. That dream was more a part of my life than my Dad. I started to curb my temper and stopped arguing back. I thought about being grateful for what I had, for the times when we did get along. I noticed that the quiet times were the ones he enjoyed the most and I tried to share them.

The Way it Was: We had a promise of a wonderful life together before the drinking and I'd hoped sobriety would mean starting over from that point in our lives. All during the first year of his sobriety, I kept quiet, never forced any issues, stuffed down all my mixed emotions, just to give us the chance to get well. I was so *nice* to him, and he was a conscientious AA member so he was *nice* to me. Everyone said I was so lucky to be his wife; he was pleasant, helpful, generous, but something was missing. It took many months to decide what I wanted to do about it; but I knew for me, love was more than patient forebearance. It wasn't enough for us just to be friendly toward one another. He made it very hard for me to leave, but I knew it was necessary. I don't think a truce can take the place of an exciting, rewarding relationship, and I cared enough about both of us to believe we both deserved better.

Uncovering Another Compulsion: When he recovered from the drinking there was still another problem. I was shocked to discover his heavy involvement in get-rich-quick schemes. I had heard others say there can be more than one compulsion—drugs, other women, gambling. He wasn't a gambler in the conventional sense, however, his habit of unrestrained spending forced us deeper and deeper in debt. I had to use the program to recover from living with a sober, charming, but totally irresponsible man as well.

New Feelings of Guilt: The fact that my wife was one drink from returning to active alcoholism put a great deal of pressure on me.

Sometimes I got the feeling that if I didn't help her recover, she would never get well. I began to feel that I was a prop, a supportive fixture; if I cracked, she'd come tumbling down. I felt guilty because I wanted her well, but I didn't want to resolve all her conflicts. She had a program and friends to help her do that. I know today I don't have to feel guilty for the way she feels about herself, and I do my best not to make her responsible for the way I feel about myself.

Dry Drunks: I had heard this expression used in reference to the behavior of a sober alcoholic which seems identical to that of active drinking days. I learned that some doctors prefer to call them "anxiety attacks" which appear to trigger patterns of behavior similar to those established in the past. Whatever the definition, these "spells," "periods in time," "stages," or "phases" seemed to be set-backs for the whole family.

The first time my daughter threw a temper tantrum in her sobriety, I wasn't ready for it. I thought, "She must have been drinking." My first reaction was to be sad: then I fell into an old habit and reacted in the same way I might have if she were drunk. I was angry. I began to yell and accuse her of all kinds of trouble-making.

When I talked it over with people who had been through this, I was somewhat relieved. They said that working the program helps us deal with "dry drunks." Getting the idea that I was supposed to be living my life through my own actions instead of my old reactions, took some doing. It was through meetings and the daily readings of Al-Anon literature that I awakened to the fact that what other people did and said reflected on *them;* what I did and said reflected on *me*. I could not be offended unless I let myself take offense. I managed to be less concerned with other people's behavior. As my daughter's recovery time lengthened, these difficult times occurred less often and were not as intense.

Slips: A return to drinking may be part of a recovery pattern or it may not. Yes, I was disappointed when my husband had a "slip" but I wasn't as afraid as I had been before. Al-Anon had helped me to live a different way and I was almost positive I could continue the new way with the loving support of my group. I learned something from that slip: one drink *did* make a difference. I was finally convinced there was no such thing as controlled drinking once the invisible line from heavy drinking to alcoholic drinking had been crossed. And I think I understand that what I do or don't do isn't the cause of the slip, either. I now believe we cannot drive another person to drink. The decision is his or hers to make. Staying sober is the responsibility of the alcoholic. I cannot enforce it.

Violence: I was afraid of my sober husband. Without booze in him, he seemed more powerful and frightening, more intolerant, even brutal. He struck out at all of us if we got in his way. The more frightened we were, the greater his rage. I was in constant fear of his outbursts. I blurted out my concern at a meeting and wasn't particularly happy to hear others speak of their similar experiences. But I did hear something that helped. There was no "rule" in Al-Anon which said I had to put up with unacceptable behavior, drunk or sober. Violence is unacceptable behavior and I was not going to let my children experience any more brutality. As their mother, I owed them, at the very least, physical safety. I took along an AA friend when I confronted my husband with my new found courage. He began therapy and is learning to work through his rages without physical force. I also sought professional care. I know today that alcohol is one of the major causes of abuse but it isn't the only one.

"Why didn't you say so?"

COMMUNICATION

Most of us who have lived with alcoholism have had trouble communicating. Unsure of what we thought and felt, we either screamed and raged or retreated into the silent worlds of fear and apprehension. Those we loved became strangers with familiar faces. Alcoholism, with its symptoms of obsession and denial, ruined all the messages we sent or received.

How do we forget what has been said or never said? How do we begin to touch when we haven't touched or when we have been touched without caring? How do we show what we think and feel when our attitudes have changed, when our spirits have awakened?

Some of us have begun to decontaminate our past communications by living one day at a time, conscious that a new Al-Anon way of thinking deserves a fresh new vocabulary, one which can be used without fear of emotional reprisal. Every word, every gesture has to have a meaning based on letting go of yesterday.

For some of us, as willing as we are to send new messages, reality will not provide a receptive partner. This may require the courage to face what can't be changed by letting others know what we think or feel.

REFLECTIONS ON

Talking and Listening: When my son came home from the rehabilitation center, I almost wrecked our new relationship. He seemed angry all the time and I wanted things to go smoothly. I would say, "You don't really feel that way, do you?" Or, "You shouldn't feel that way." When I spoke at an Al-Anon meeting about my reaction to his behavior, members suggested I try to accept him as he is, to listen to what he has to say without having all the answers. At a meeting on the Third Step I began to see that it wasn't my job to educate or train my son anymore. He was an adult and I would have to allow him to change his own attitudes, when and if he cared to. Now I think I am lucky when my son tells me how he feels. I try to tell him how I feel, too, although I know he's not always going to like hearing what I have to say.

Ignoring Bad Language: Sometimes people say one thing and mean another. Frustrations and fears are often disguised with angry words. Nothing is gained by dwelling on phrases or words which are hurled at me. I forget insults because they are meaningless, but I do say I don't like them. I do have the choice to listen or not listen to someone who is insulting.

Pouting: Covering up anger with silence never solved a disagreement for me. Some of my arguments ended when I realized I was keeping quiet, waiting to be asked, "What's the matter?" Then I could really say what was bothering me. When I took my inventory, I saw that I was using silence to get my way, without having to go on record by saying anything. This way, everyone had to guess how they made me angry. I took the Fifth Step with an Al-Anon friend and tried to clean out old hurts in order to stop using silence as a weapon.

Telling a Story: In Al-Anon we tell our own story, not the alcoholic's. In any situation, it isn't a good idea to bring up a loved one's mistakes, boorish behavior, accidents, etc. At AA meetings, alcoholics tell stories about their drinking days but *they* are the storytellers. Because I recognize my friend's sensitivity in this area, I try only to tell how the drinking affected me. I care about his feelings and I respect them. He doesn't always return the favor, but I don't think that should be a reason for being less considerate.

Asking: I was at my wit's end when after several years of sobriety, my roommate would disappear whenever there was work to be done or some problem to be solved. I tried not to judge his lack of responsibility, but finally I couldn't stand it another day. I practiced saying what I wanted to change. I didn't cloud up the situation with resentments about AA activity. I just said, "I'm fed up with doing all the work around here because I have to take too big a share in the chores that make our home run smoothly." I braced myself for a counter-attack. There was none. He said, "O.K." and we sat down and talked over the jobs and how best to share them. After years of resentments, we worked out a schedule which was acceptable to us both. I could have kicked myself for not speaking up sooner.

Assuming: Mind readers are in the minority. How can we expect another person to know what we're thinking about if we don't tell him? And yet, I was so ready to assume I knew what the alcoholic was thinking. It was with the help of the program that I became willing to wait for others to express themselves without anticipating their words.

Being Expressive: We talked in telegrams; all that passed between us was bits of information: "The car is ready, the plumber will be here on Tuesday." I was afraid to talk about anything important because I thought she'd say, "I don't love you, I'm leaving." At meetings I asked, "How am I supposed to begin?" "What and how do I say it?" My friends urged me to have courage and to relax. One member said my telegrams were at least part of communication. We were exchanging information. I then tried to expand the messages. I made positive declarations, "I enjoyed the casserole." That's not terribly profound but I was able to say how I felt. Later, I said, "I like the way you smile," because I did and today we can honestly say we like each other.

Honest Expressions of Feelings: There is a difference between honest expressions of feeling and making the person I love be the waste basket for all my bad feelings. I think I'm encouraged by the program to take my own inventory so that I can do something about my discoveries rather than expect someone else to take care of them. If I make an effort, I can express myself without making others responsible for the way I feel, and I can be truthful without being brutal or indiscreet.

No Retribution: I used the Tenth Step as a guide each day to rediscover who I was and what I wanted others to know about me. It was important to let the people I loved know who I was trying to be. Al-Anon gave me a new perspective and I wanted the chance to be listened to. I resolved to talk the way I wished to be talked to: courteously and pleasantly. I was equally adamant about how I listened: patiently, without picking out words and phrases to pounce on. I refused to argue at first. I would say, "I think I'm getting too worked up to talk this over with you; let's try later." We began to say things without being afraid we were going to be punished somehow for what we thought.

Body Language: I heard so much talk about communication at meetings. I was sure we weren't having any; but if you asked me, I was able to tell you just what he was thinking. I could see it in his face, tell it in the way he flexed his back muscles, and feel it in the icy silences which would follow something I did or said. I had a series of signals, myself. I remember one which made him particularly angry. I used to hold up my hand in the classic traffic "stop" position. I realized we were developing a silent language-of-signs and that we were coming close to clenched fists. It wasn't at my Al-Anon meetings that I learned how or what to say, but what I did learn there was to think better of myself and have the courage to try the spoken word.

Silence: I talked like a machine gun. To get some kind of reaction from a sober but silent loved one, I tried every word I had ever heard. I wanted to reach some part of that center in that human being, and I hoped there would be a nod or two which could let me stop talking. Inevitably I would say too much and I would have to start all over again on another topic, waiting for some acknowledgment that I was forgiven. Finally, I began to understand I was battling the silences, not communicating anything but noise. I endured long periods of quiet before he began to believe I wasn't going to fill a void just to break the silence. An improvement in my self-image has helped me to enjoy quiet without resenting it. I believe that I now accept another person's right to reflection. As long as I feel secure, the silence can belong to me, too.

Speaking Another Language: Her vocabulary was different from mine. She'd say, "Come watch TV with me." I wanted her to say, "I want to be with you tonight because I love you," because that's what I needed to hear. It was several months before it occurred to me that we didn't use the same words to say the same things. I don't know why this came as such a shock to me. We had met and courted in our mother tongue but I became aware of this difference in expression as I went to meetings and listened. I knew I didn't feel bad if members said things using their own terms, and yet, I felt unhappy because this woman I loved didn't say what I wanted to hear. I began to translate: When she said, "Come watch TV with me," she was really saying, "I want you to be with me." After awhile I was able to get the message, and the chosen words didn't matter as much.

Risking Disapproval: I handled sobriety by avoiding confrontation—at a terrible cost to myself. In order to avoid the emotional expense of my spouse's disapproval, I paid an even higher price in never getting to know what *I* really thought: who I was or what I wanted to do with my life. No one has the right to impose his will on another adult human being. Just as I must watch to see that I don't do it to anyone else, I must not permit it to be done to me. When another's efforts to control me (by imposing guilt, by withholding approval, by exuding anger) no longer work, he gives them up; but he has no reason to let go of them as long as they are so beautifully effective, has he?

Loving: I learned more about loving from my friends than I had ever been taught by my alcoholic parents. As a recovering alcoholic, I had joined Al-Anon when my wife continued to drink excessively, after I had stopped. It was there that I learned about family life for the first time: loving without conditions, loyalty as opposed to obsession. The product of an alcoholic home, I hadn't known about these moments of total sharing.

Loving: For me, love means giving and getting comfort, care and compassion; for others there can be no love without dignity and shared responsibility. For some, feelings die when they are not returned in kind, nurtured and protected by an attentive partner. Others can love unconditionally, but from a distance. The capacity for loving may exceed a partner's capacity or it may not. Whatever our feelings may be, they are neither bad nor good; they simply are, and we have to work with them. I am free to love whomever I choose, and love, freely given, is the most rewarding.

Love: My feelings are changing. I let time help me sort them out. Today, I know what it is to love and that is enough for me. Working on removing my defects of character gives me less time to brood about the quality of love I am receiving and more time in improving the quality of love I am giving.

Loving: I don't think you can learn to love someone, but I do think it is possible to learn how to be more loving. If I can improve my conscious contact with a Higher Power through prayer and meditation, I can improve conscious contact with people through communication and thoughtfulness. I became aware of others through regular attendance at meetings, and I learned to listen and appreciate how others were able to express themselves. I learned tolerance and acceptance and these concepts helped me to be more loving. I am letting go of the past, trying to live one day at a time with an open and receptive attitude. There were great spaces in me, areas where resentment and fear had lived, and I tried to fill them with warm and positive thoughts. I remind myself to reach out and hug my children; I ask them to hug me back.

Loving: The miracle to me is that *any* relationship survives sobriety, not that so many do. Think of it! After sobriety, the alcoholic looks at us without the haze of alcohol blurring his mental vision; he experiences us with no anesthetic to soften the sharp edges; and we, who are Al-Anons, are forced to live in reality, to give up the fantasies with which we had thickly overlaid the barren facts of our lives. I deplore the feelings I pick up here and there that anyone whose relationship has ended after the program has somehow flunked Al-Anon or AA. Neither fellowship makes any claim at all to save our marriages or our love affairs—only our sanity. Al-Anon is not meant to be a therapeutic tool for my relationships. It is for my growth, my recovery and that, I think, leads to healthy relationships.

Sex: We were both self-conscious about sex after sobriety, we spoiled what might have been a wonderful closeness. I think there were leftovers from my childhood days, too. I disliked my father for his drunken demands and I carried that feeling into all my relationships. I had to take an inventory with professional help.

Sex: My wife was physically shy when she was sober. It was very difficult for me to understand her reluctance to be touched, especially, since I seemed to thrive on open expressions of affection. Of all the ways humans have to communicate, I felt sex was the most personal and yet I didn't know how to handle her sober rejection of me. After a meeting, I spoke to several close friends about this difficulty in our relationship. They assured me this wasn't a unique situation; some of their experiences were similar. I decided a good sex life was worth some patience and tolerance. I resolved to work on bettering our verbal communication before losing hope in physical contact.

Sex: I talked to many people and read everything I could on sexual inadequacy. I knew that alcohol affected some people adversely and made others feel amorous, but I was convinced that it had destroyed my husband's interest in sex. In a moment of rare courage, I asked him about his feelings. He said he was still interested in sex, but although he was very fond of me, he just wasn't interested in sex *with me*. He said he would be happy to continue a platonic relationship. I decided marriage was incomplete without a sexual partner. My decision was reached with calm and serenity, and I think he was relieved that I had the courage to end our marriage rather than continue to ask him to give what he was unable to give to me.

Sex: My sober husband called me a prude. When I confided this to a friend after an Al-Anon meeting, she asked, "Are you?" I had looked for sympathy and instead I had been challenged to look at myself. All the way home from that meeting I asked myself, "Am I a prude?" and I couldn't answer. We had married when we were teenagers and the drinking began soon after. I recalled that much of our early life together was spoiled for me by the way he looked and smelled when he was drunk, but I also knew that many of my adult thoughts and actions were the result of attitudes I had been taught by my parents. I asked my husband to be patient while I sought counseling to help dispel some of the myths about sex which I had accepted as truths. I also continued to use the program to rid myself of the resentments from the drinking days. Because neither of us wanted to use sex as a weapon, we have a better marriage today.

Sex: My lover's desire for me ended with sobriety. I was heartbroken. I couldn't understand why such a thing could happen. I took his impotency personally, just as I had with other difficulties. I couldn't understand—I watched my weight, dressed well, looked attractive—why did this happen? I knew an Al-Anon meeting wasn't a sex therapy unit, but members would often indicate some problems in this sensitive area of interaction between loved ones. I had the courage to speak to a member after the meeting, and with discretion and candor we talked about impotency and alcoholism. He offered his experience that it isn't unusual for alcohol to render one partner incapable, and that impotency and other kinds of sexual inadequacy also occur in sobriety. I was relieved to learn that it wasn't a problem I had created. I tried not to compound the situation. Sex wasn't the only reason I loved this man, and I knew I would have to allow him the opportunity to take care of this problem. I waited with love and patience for him to seek help. Unfortunately, he refused to even talk about the subject and, in time, I had to face the probability that ours would be a sexless relationship. My acceptance of it was based on my own needs as well as my love for him.

Sex: I worked on my physical appearance as well as my outlook. Let's face it. If we develop enough self-esteem to avoid demanding or complaining approaches; if we care enough about ourselves to be the most attractive we can be, we are more likely to command attention.

Sex: I feel that sexual activity in consenting adults requires awareness of the highest order. It helps to have participants who are interested, interesting and able. Some of my friends felt reluctant to renew a physical relationship with a newly-sobered alcoholic whom they didn't know anymore. Others have related the anguish they experienced when they became aware of the sexual infidelities of their spouse. Some were able to resolve their difficulties and some were not.

"Happiness takes some getting used to."

HAPPINESS

There is more to happiness than our memory of it. The feeling we get when we actively experience a joyous moment today exceeds the feeling of comfort we try to create by remembering when we used to be happy. As living, breathing creatures, our most intense sensations are being experienced NOW, this moment, this is our reality. Memories are not real. We remember what we want and need to remember, and often, if we aren't comfortable thinking of life as it really was, we rearrange the facts by using our imagination.

Those of us who have lived with alcoholism know what it is to daydream. Our fantasies were legion. Our "pretend" partners were kind, generous, supportive and sober—and, ah yes, they made us happy. Of course, they had a tendency to fade away if our thoughts were interrupted. To keep our dreams alive, we had to keep reality from intruding, to cut ourselves off from an awareness of life and to reduce our involvement to passive images of what-might-have-been.

To be happy today, we have to let go of our shadow worlds. For most of us in Al-Anon, this is made possible through considerable spiritual effort, one which we need to make whether or not the alcoholic finds continuing sobriety.

Those of us who are interested in making another beginning have to surrender the daydreams and begin with what is real. We try not to make comparisons with our past visions of perfection. Our Al-Anon experience tells us: we can not expect or ask others to make us happy; each of us is essentially responsible for his own thoughts and actions; our happiness is an outward expression of our inner spiritual health; we all have the right to be happy; how, when and where is up to us.

REFLECTIONS ON

Serenity: I said the Serenity Prayer long before I believed in a Higher Power. When my parents were drinking, I said it just to keep myself from falling apart. It made me calm. After a while, I came to believe that a Higher Power whom I chose to call God was going to take care of all of us. I really became confident. God was planning a party for me but I would have to get ready for it; I would have to be willing to learn to be happy. I began by thinking "happy"; I tried to catch myself whenever I had dark thoughts or used grim language. I practiced smiling, walking without dragging my feet, and working on being less intense and more playful. I think today that I have serenity-plus.

Using the Program: Through the years of living with a sober alcoholic, I have continued to go to meetings. The effects of alcoholism were devastating to my sense of well-being and the recovery tools offered by the Al-Anon program continue to restore me. I know living one day at a time with a new attitude and understanding gives me a way to get through my set of personal problems today. What I receive from listening to the experiences of others, the way they use the Steps, the slogans, etc., is not so much *how* they have managed but that they *have* managed to turn their lives around. It hasn't always been easy or pleasant to live with a recovering alcoholic. It has been very difficult for me to accept him as he is when there are still traces of behavior which lessen the quality of our lives together, but I choose to stay with him because I am happy being with him a majority of the time. The rest of the time, I can say I am happy being with me.

Gratitude: My happiness depends on my ability to recognize the beauty and goodness which surround me. When I was able to see what a lucky guy I was, I began to know what it could mean to be happy again. I am lucky for many reasons; one of them is that my wife is sober; and I'm grateful that I found a program which gives me the tools to live my life one day at a time. I am grateful for being introduced to the concept of a Higher Power who I believe is helping me to allow myself to be happy. Being happy takes some getting used to. I think I had forgotten how to be happy. Sometimes I felt I didn't deserve to be, but now I appreciate what I do have and try not to spoil my happiness with self-pity or regrets.

Maturity: Today, I am my own mother and father. Being mature asks me to be for myself, what most parents are for their children. I think mature people make the best partners, and most of the people I know who live happily with other people have discovered several mature attitudes. They have a willingness and grace to offer each other courtesy, kindness and acceptance; they are not crushed by the weight of each other's moods or depressions; they resist the temptation to offer solutions for their loved one's problems or make decisions for them; they do not depend on each other for emotional stability; they make allowances for each other's interests and hobbies; they share their belongings, responsibilities, freedom to express their feelings, trust, time and effort, and comfortable silences; they are happy being together or by themselves; they are not trying to be all things to all people.

Responsibility: I know I'm not responsible for another person's happiness. My contribution to a person's pleasant experiences may be appreciated or it may not, but if I do not take the responsibility or the credit for making anyone else happy, then I cannot expect that their actions are responsible for my happiness. I alone can be as happy as I want to be.

Faith: I believe there is more to life than the problems it presents. There is more to life than alcoholism and recovery from the effects of that disease. There is more to life than being emotionally and physically comfortable. I believe I need to be willing to have a recovery of spirit. I want to grow in my willingness to make room in my life for good times, having faith in their arrival and patience in my anticipation.

ANOTHER BEGINNING

There is no attempt here to define a happy ending. What would it be? What could it be for all of us? Our shared reflections tell us that it is not measured by others, nor is it calculated by continued sobriety in those we love. While sobriety in others can be a welcome miracle, it doesn't guarantee our happiness.

For the men, women, and children in Al-Anon/Alateen today, happiness appears to lie in a willingness to concentrate on recovering from the effects of living with alcoholism, whether or not the alcoholic recovers. This means, if we are to recover, we need to be free of our past fears and resentments, capable of dealing with our fears and feelings of guilt, confident of who we are, able to express ourselves to others, and spiritually able to enjoy life today.

It would seem, then, there is no point where we stop in our efforts to find emotional balance and spiritual peace. Each event simply adds another dimension to our lives and while sobriety in others may offer us an opportunity to rejoice, it is not the end of our search; but it can be another beginning.

INDEX